COCKTAILS
&
BAR DRINKS

Hodder & Stoughton
A MEMBER OF THE HODDER HEADLINE GROUP

Cataloguing in Publication Data is available from the British Library

ISBN 0 340 65872 X

First edition 1990
Second edition 1996

Impression number   10   9   8   7   6   5   4   3   2   1
Year   2000   1999   1998   1997   1996

Typeset by Wearset, Boldon, Tyne and Wear.
Printed in Hong Kong for Hodder & Stoughton Educational,
a division of Hodder Headline Plc, 338 Euston Road,
London NW1 3BH by Colorcraft Ltd, Hong Kong.

$\mathcal{I}$NTRODUCTION

This book has been designed as a functional, indispensable manual for all cocktail makers and bar-tenders. It provides:

- a wide variety of alcoholic and non-alcoholic drinks to suit all ages, tastes and occasions
- an alphabetical index for quick reference
- a drink on every page
- clear, concise instructions
- a colour photograph per drink for perfect presentation
- colour coding according to the main ingredient for easy cocktail selection suggestion
- an essential 'aide-mémoire' for professional bar-tenders and hosts/hostesses alike

Cocktails and Bar Drinks is a vital ingredient for all successful cocktail makers. Home entertainers will find it invaluable in selecting, preparing and presenting cocktails and drinks for those special events. It will also be useful for hotel and catering managers, trainees, students, bar staff, steward and stewardesses throughout the entire industry. In particular *Cocktails and Bar Drinks* will be invaluable to all students studying on S/NVQ Programmes, Level 1, 2 and 3, GNVQ Intermediate and Advanced, HNC and Higher National Diploma, for examinations leading to membership of the HCIMA and for Limited Skill Certificates, Caterbase programmes and Degree level courses.

COCKTAILS

Contents

A brief history

Cocktails are the designer drink of today, with a wide choice to suit every age, taste and occasion. The origin of the word 'cocktail' is unclear, but there are numerous suggestions:

- *Coquetel* a mixed drink from the Bordeaux region of France, served to French officers serving in the USA
- *Cock-ale* a mixture of spirits given to fighting cocks in the eighteenth century in England and used as a toast to the victorious bird
- *Cock-tailed* the docking of horse's tail to indicate a horse of mixed stock – a cocktail – not a thoroughbred
- *Coquetiers* a type of egg cup used by a French physician to serve his mixed drinks to American friends
- *Vive le cocktail* Betsy Flanagan, an Irish tavern keeper in USA, served mixed drinks from bottles decorated with cocks feathers; a Frenchman in proposing a toast declared "Vive le cocktail!"

Without a doubt, whatever the origin, everyone agrees that the Cocktail Age started in earnest in the Prohibition Era in USA 1920–1933. It was an ingenious idea to mix several drinks together and so disguise the doubtful origins, aromas and purity of illicit liquor. Prohibition was repealed in 1933 and liquor standards raised, so cocktail creations and contents became more refined. Cocktails became respectable and have continued to improve and develop to become the drinking vogue for all.

Cocktails range from elegant 'classics' (Dry Martini, Manhattan and Sidecar) to the fun, colourful, exotic creations (Harvey Wallbanger, Pinacolada, and Tequila Sunrise). Cocktails are associated with glamour, style and charisma.

The measure

All measures listed use the professional bar measure called a 'Jigger', which can be purchased in 25 ml and 50 ml size – a worthwhile investment for the cocktail maker. Alternatively, the

25 ml measure can be replaced by the use of a liqueur glass.

All cocktails listed are for one serving.

Measures quoted may be increased or decreased but *ratios* of ingredients should remain constant.

Glassware

Glassware for cocktails varies in shape, size and character. A well mixed drink will taste good in which ever glass it is served, but custom dictates that certain drinks are more appropriately served in certain shaped glasses. Generally this is due to the quantity and mixture of the drink.

It is important that all glassware is scrupulously clean and sparkling. To check for cleanliness, the selected glass should be held up to the light and repolished with a dry, fine linen cloth if necessary. It should then be held up to the light and rechecked.

Cocktails taste better when served ice cold. Chill the glass by filling it with ice cubes and soda water whilst preparing the cocktail. The glass is then emptied just prior to pouring the cocktail.

In this book the most suitable glass has been selected for each cocktail. The glassware used is listed below.

Brandy balloon

Short stemmed balloon bowl glass, wide at base and narrow at rim. The shape allows for the full aroma of the drink to be trapped and appreciated.

Champagne saucer

A stemmed glass with a wide saucer-shaped bowl; its shape allows excess bubbles from sparkling wines to escape. Sometimes referred to as a 'champagne coupe'.

Cocktail glass

Designed with the cocktail drinker in mind, it has a long slim stem for ease of holding. The warmth of the hand does not therefore warm the cocktail and detract from the quality and taste. The curved shaped bowl creates style and character.

Collins (10 fluid ounce)

Tall, straight-sided tumbler for those extra-long cocktails, eg Zombies, Collins.

Highball (8 fluid ounce)

Tall straight-sided tumbler used for long cocktails, eg Cuba Libre, Punches, Noggs, Pimms.

Lowball (5 fluid ounce)

Short tumbler with sloping sides. Used for Bloody Mary and other similar drinks.

Martini glass

Stemmed glass with 'V' shaped bowl. An elegant glass for classics such as Martinis and Daiquiri.

Old Fashioned (8 fluid ounce)

Tumbler with sloping sides. Used for Mists, Gibson, Americano etc.

Paris goblet

Short stemmed, round bowled standard wine glass. Ideal for Black Velvet, Prairie Oyster.

Sour glass (5 fluid ounce)

Stemmed glass with tall, slim bowl that curves in slightly at rim. This allows sparkling drinks to retain effervescent for longer.

Equipment

Cocktail shaker

Made of stainless steel or silver in three sections:

(a) the base for ingredients
(b) a top with built-in strainer which fits tightly over the base
(c) a cap which covers the top, allowing the cocktail to be shaken

The strained cocktail is poured from the shaker into the appropriate glass.

Note: cocktails are stirred when all the ingredients are clear.

Mixing glass

Used for stirred cocktails. A glass jug without a handle, but with a lip for easy pouring. Requires use of a hawthorn strainer to strain the cocktail into the correct glass.

Hawthorn strainer

Stainless steel or silver flat short-handled strainer with spring coiled on exterior. This allows for tight fitting in the top of the mixing glass or glass section of a Boston shaker.

Barspoon

Spiralled, long-handled teaspoon with flat muddler end. The muddler is used for crushing sugar and mint as necessary.

Blender

Used especially for drinks containing puréed fruits or for preparing large quantities of a particular cocktail.

Measures

A 'Jigger' or measure is a means of measuring and controlling the quantity of liquid ingredients. A Jigger, combining the 25 ml and the 50 ml measures, is a must to ensure the consistency of the selected cocktail.

Additional useful equipment

The following useful equipment should be readily available in a truly professional cocktail bar:

Waiter's friend/corkscrew: for opening bottles
Bottle stopper: for sealing opened bottles of sparkling wine
Ice buckets: for storage of ice cubes (plentiful supply essential)
Ice tongs: for hygienic dispensing of ice
Ice crusher: for easy preparation from ice cubes
Chopping board/working surfaces: for garnish preparation
Bar knife: for preparing garnishes; tonged end for 'picking up' garnish
Canelle knife: for removing zest for garnish
Teaspoon: for measuring ingredient
Juice extractor: for fresh fruit juice preparation
Crown cork opener: for removing bottle tops
Wine cooler: for champagne chilling
Fine linen cloths: for glassware polishing
Bar mats: to absorb moisture/spillage from bar top

Paper goods

Paper goods are used to enhance the presentation of the cocktail:

Swizzle stick: for stirring drinks
Coasters: for underneath the cocktail glass
Cocktail napkins: for drinker's convenience
Cocktail sticks: for presenting cocktail garnishes
Straws: of assorted colours, lengths, sizes and shapes
Doyleys: for perfect presentation when using underplates for cocktail service
Parasols: for exotic, fun, colourful presentation

Ingredients

The majority of the cocktails in this book are based on the following main ingredients: gin, vodka, rum, whisky, wine, vermouth, and other various spirits and minerals (in the case of non-alcoholic drinks).

Additional extras

Miscellaneous ingredients should be plentiful and on hand to enable an efficient cocktail service to be offered. These additional extras can be displayed on silver salvers on bar tops to help promote cocktail sales.

The most frequently used ingredients include: olives, cocktail onions, salt and pepper, nutmeg (grated), tabasco sauce, cayenne pepper, Worcester sauce, tomato ketchup, Angostura bitters, sugar syrup (gomme), grenadine syrup, almond syrup (orgeat), rosewater, castor sugar, sugar cubes, coffee beans, eggs, milk, cream, yoghurt, raisins, honey, tea, coconut cream.

Garnishes

Garnishes should be stored correctly to maintain perfect
condition. They should be prepared only to order to retain their
crispness, freshness and juiciness.

A garnish should be appropriate for the selected cocktail,
according to the ingredients, and should be used to create a
good, balanced, visual impression. It should not be used to
overdress a cocktail or cause embarrassment or inconvenience to
the drinker. Garnishes should enhance a cocktail and create an
exotic drink experience.

Garnishes used include: cocktail cherries, lemons, limes,
oranges, pineapple, coconut, apples, mint, kiwi fruit,
strawberries, mint and cucumber.

A garnish is the final colourful touch which completes the
selected cocktail. Cocktails can be dressed up with:

Fruit: which is cut into different shapes and thicknesses: slices, triangles, semi-circles, slithers, zest spirals, twists
Mint leaves: which should be lightly crushed to impart flavour (as should citrus peel)
Cucumber skin: which is best peeled to extract the delicate flavour
Cocktail cherries: which are available in various colours, the natural red being the most versatile

Garnish preparation allows for individual creativity and ingenuity.

Making cocktails

'Frosting' glassware

Dip the rim of glass in egg white or lemon juice. Redip in castor sugar or salt. Tidy up 'frosting' if required.

It is usual to 'frost' with sugar those cocktails containing a neutral spirit, ie gin, vodka, white rum. 'Salt frosting' does not appeal to all drinkers.

Checklist

1 Prepare all necessary glassare, ingredients and garnishes. Chill glassare if required
2 Half fill shaker or bar glass with ice and add ingredients
3 Shake or stir vigorously. Never shake any effervescent ingredient
4 Strain carefully into prepared glassware
5 Add garnishes and serve

Shake, stir or pour?

A cocktail is a skilfully blended drink prepared by shaking, stirring or pouring to create an exotic drink experience. It is the ingredients that determine the method:

Shake
(Using a cocktail shaker)
Fruit juice, egg white, egg yolk, cream, milk, or any cloudy ingredient

Stir
(Using a bar glass)
All clear ingredients

Pour
(Using specified presentation glass)
Ingredients of different specific gravities when separate distinct layers are required

Recipes

𝒜LEXANDER

RATIOS	INGREDIENTS
1	1 × 25ml brandy
1	1 × 25ml crème de cacao
1	1 × 25ml cream
	crushed ice
	grated nutmeg

PREPARATION

¼ fill shaker with crushed ice
Add all ingredients
Shake well
Strain into small cocktail glass
Sprinkle with grated nutmeg

$\mathscr{A}$U REVOIR

RATIOS
1
1

INGREDIENTS
1 × 25ml brandy
1 × 25ml sloe gin
juice of 1 lemon
1 egg white
1 lemon slice
4 ice cubes

PREPARATION
Place ice cubes in shaker
Add brandy, sloe gin, lemon juice and egg white
Shake well and strain
Pour into cocktail glass
Garnish with lemon slice

𝐵ETWEEN THE SHEETS

RATIOS	INGREDIENTS
1	½ × 25ml white rum
1	½ × 25ml brandy
1	½ × 25ml Cointreau
	1 teaspoon lemon juice
	lemon twist
	ice cubes

PREPARATION

Place ice cubes in shaker
Add all ingredients
Shake well and strain
Serve in chilled cocktail glass
Garnish with lemon twist

*B*OSOM CARESSER

RATIOS	INGREDIENTS
2	2 × 25ml brandy
1	1 × 25ml orange Curaçao
	4 dashes grenadine
	1 egg yolk
	2 fresh cherries
	5 ice cubes

PREPARATION
Place ice cubes in shaker
Add grenadine, egg yolk, brandy and orange Curaçao
Shake well and strain
Serve in chilled champagne saucer
Garnish with cherries

*C*OFFEE

RATIOS	INGREDIENTS
3	1½ × 25ml brandy
1	½ × 25ml port
	1 teaspoon sugar
	1 egg yolk
	4 ice cubes
	coffee beans

PREPARATION

Place ice cubes in shaker
Add brandy, port, sugar and egg yolk
Shake well
Strain into old fashioned glass
Garnish with coffee beans

𝒞UBAN COCKTAIL

RATIOS	**INGREDIENTS**
2	1 × 25ml brandy
1	½ × 25ml apricot brandy
	juice of ½ lemon
	5 ice cubes
	1 slice kiwi fruit

PREPARATION
Place ice cubes in shaker
Add lemon juice, brandy and apricot brandy
Shake well and strain
Pour into chilled cocktail glass
Garnish with kiwi fruit

$\mathscr{H}$ORSE'S NECK

RATIOS	INGREDIENTS
1	1 × 25ml brandy
4	11.3cl ginger ale
	1 lemon spiral
	2 ice cubes

PREPARATION

Place ice cubes in highball glass
Add brandy and spiral of lemon peel
Top with ginger ale

*S*IDECAR

RATIOS	**INGREDIENTS**
1	1 × 25ml brandy
1	1 × 25ml Cointreau
1	1 × 25ml lemon juice, crushed ice
	1 orange slice, 1 lemon slice,
	1 cocktail cherry, 1 cocktail stick

PREPARATION

Fill shaker ¾ full with crushed ice
Add brandy, Cointreau and lemon juice
Shake well and strain. Serve in chilled cocktail glass
Garnish with orange, lemon and cherry on stick

One of classics associated with Harry's New York Bar, Paris in 1911.
Invented for a customer who arrived at the bar in a sidecar.

ℐTINGER

RATIOS	**INGREDIENTS**
3	1½ × 25ml brandy
1	½ × 25ml white crème de menthe
	sprigs of mint
	8–9 ice cubes

PREPARATION

Place ice cubes in shaker
Add crème de menthe and brandy
Shake well and strain
Serve in chilled brandy balloon
Garnish with mint

*A*DELAIDE

RATIOS	INGREDIENTS
1	1 × 25ml gin
1	1 × 25ml sweet vermouth
1	1 × 25ml lime juice (fresh in possible)
	3 dashes grenadine
	1 tablespoon crushed ice
	1 slice lime or lemon

PREPARATION

Place crushed ice in bar glass
Pour gin, vermouth and lime juice over ice
Add grenadine
Stir and strain
Serve in chilled cocktail glass
Garnish with slice of fresh lime or lemon

*B*LUE ARROW

RATIOS	INGREDIENTS
2	1 × 25ml gin
1	½ × 25ml Cointreau
1	½ × 25ml lime juice
1	½ × 25ml blue Curaçao
	crushed ice

PREPARATION

Fill shaker ¾ full with crushed ice
Add gin, Cointreau, lime juice and Curaçao
Shake well and strain
Serve in chilled cocktail glass

*B*RONX

RATIOS	INGREDIENTS
2	1 × 25ml gin
1	½ × 25ml sweet vermouth
1	½ × 25ml dry vermouth
1	½ × 25ml orange juice
	2 tablespoons crushed ice
	1 cocktail cherry, 1 cocktail stick

PREPARATION

Place crushed ice in shaker
Add gin, sweet and dry vermouth and orange juice
Shake well and strain
Serve in chilled Martini glass
Garnish with cherry on stick

*C*LOVER CLUB

RATIOS   **INGREDIENTS**

1   1 × 25ml gin

               6 dashes grenadine

1   1 × 25ml lemon juice

               1 egg white

               crushed ice

PREPARATION

Fill shaker ¾ full with crushed ice

Add gin, grenadine, lemon juice and egg white

Shake well

Strain into chilled cocktail glass

*D*UBONNET COCKTAIL

RATIOS   **INGREDIENTS**
1   1 × 25ml gin
1   1 × 25ml Dubonnet
                1 lemon rind
                6 ice cubes

PREPARATION

Place ice cubes in bar glass
Add Dubonnet and gin
Stir well and strain
Serve into cocktail glass
Add twist of lemon rind

𝒢IBSON

Ratios	**Ingredients**
3	1½ × 25ml gin
1	½ × 25ml extra dry sherry
	1 cocktail onion, 1 cocktail stick, 5 ice cubes

Preparation

Place ice cubes in bar glass
Pour on sherry and gin
Stir well
Strain into chilled old fashioned glass
Garnish with cocktail onion on stick

Invented for the artist Charles Dana Gibson by Charley Connelly, bartender at the Player's Club, New York during prohibition.

*G*IMLET

RATIOS	INGREDIENTS
2	1 × 50ml gin
1	1 × 25ml bottled lime juice
	2 tablespoons crushed ice
	1 lime wheel
	straws

PREPARATION

Place crushed ice in shaker
Add lime juice and gin
Shake well and strain
Serve in chilled cocktail glass
Garnish with lime wheel and straws

*G*IN SLING

RATIOS	**INGREDIENTS**
3	1½ × 25ml gin
1	½ × 25ml cherry brandy
1	½ × 25ml lemon juice
	soda, 1 lemon slice, 6 ice cubes
	1 cocktail cherry, 1 cocktail stick, straws

PREPARATION

Place ice cubes, lemon juice, cherry brandy and gin in shaker
Shake well and strain. Pour into highball glass
Top up with soda
Garnish with lemon and cherry on stick and straws

*The only survivor of the category of cocktails known as 'Slings' – could
be made with any spirit. Similar to a Collins.*

*G*IN SOUR

RATIOS	**INGREDIENTS**
3	1½ × 25ml gin
1	½ × 25ml lemon juice
	3 dashes gomme (sugar syrup)
	1 cocktail cherry
	1 cocktail stick
	1 lemon slice
	6 ice cubes

PREPARATION

Place ice cubes in shaker
Pour on lemon juice, sugar syrup and gin
Shake well and strain
Serve in sour glass
Garnish with cherry on stick and lemon slice

JOHN COLLINS

RATIOS	INGREDIENTS
3	3 × 25ml gin
1	1 × 25ml lemon juice
	1 teaspoon gomme (sugar syrup)
	180ml soda, 1 lemon slice
	1 sprig of mint, 6 ice cubes

PREPARATION

Place ice cubes in shaker. Pour in sugar syrup
Add lemon juice and gin
Shake well. Pour into chilled highball glass
Top up with soda. Stir gently
Garnish with mint and lemon slice

Named after John Collins, head waiter at Limmers, London. John Collins (Dry gin), Tom Collins (Old Tom Gin).

MARTINI (DRY)

RATIOS	INGREDIENTS
3	1½ × 25ml gin
1	½ × 25ml dry vermouth
	4 ice cubes
	1 olive, 1 cocktail stick

PREPARATION
Place ice cubes in bar glass
Add gin and dry vermouth
Stir well. Strain into Martini glass
Garnish with olive on stick

Named after the bartender at the Knickerbocker Hotel, New York 1910
— the King of Cocktails — most international of all cocktails.

$\mathcal{M}$ARTINI (MEDIUM)

RATIOS	INGREDIENTS
1	⅓ × 50ml gin
1	⅓ × 50ml dry vermouth
1	⅓ × 50ml sweet vermouth
	8 ice cubes

PREPARATION

Place ice cubes in bar glass
Add gin and dry and sweet vermouths
Stir well and strain
Serve in chilled Martini glass
No garnish

$\mathcal{M}$ARTINI (SWEET)

RATIOS	INGREDIENTS
1	1 × 25ml gin
1	1 × 25ml sweet vermouth
	8 ice cubes
	1 cocktail cherry
	1 cocktail stick

PREPARATION

Place ice cubes in bar glass
Add gin and sweet vermouth
Stir well and strain
Serve in chilled Martini glass
Garnish with cocktail cherry on stick

ORANGE BLOSSOM

RATIOS   **INGREDIENTS**

1   1 × 50ml gin

1   1 × 50ml orange juice

               2 dashes Angostura bitters

               1 sprig of mint, crushed ice

               orange twist, 1 slice cucumber

PREPARATION

Fill shaker ¾ full with crushed ice

Add Angostura bitters, gin and orange juice

Shake and strain

Pour into chilled cocktail glass

Garnish with sprig of mint if available or orange twist and
cucumber

*P*INK GIN

RATIOS	INGREDIENTS
1	1 × 25ml gin
	1 dash Angostura bitters
2	2 × 25ml iced water

PREPARATION

Place Angostura bitters in Paris goblet and swill around glass
Add gin
Top up with iced water

Associated with the officers of the Royal Navy. Was probably invented in the West Indies.

$\mathscr{P}$INK LADY

RATIOS	INGREDIENTS
1	1 × 25ml gin
1	1 × 25ml calvados
1	1 × 25ml lime juice
	5 dashes grenadine
	crushed ice, 1 slice of lime
	1 cocktail cherry, 1 cocktail stick

PREPARATION

Fill shaker ½ full with crushed ice
Add gin, calvados, lime juice and grenadine
Shake well and strain
Pour into sugar frosted cocktail glass
Garnish with lime and cocktail cherry on stick

*W*HITE LADY

RATIOS	INGREDIENTS
1	1 × 25ml gin
1	1 × 25ml Cointreau
1	1 × 25ml lemon juice
	crushed ice, 1 lemon slice
	1 cocktail cherry, 1 cocktail stick

PREPARATION

Fill shaker ¾ full with crushed ice
Add gin, Cointreau and lemon juice
Shake well and strain
Serve in chilled cocktail glass
Garnish with lemon slice and cherry on stick

Another creation from Harry's New York Bar, Paris.

*B*ACARDI

RATIOS	**INGREDIENTS**
1	1½ × 25ml Cuban rum
1	juice of 1 lime
	2 dashes grenadine, 1 cocktail cherry
	lemon slice, 1 cocktail stick, 4 ice cubes

PREPARATION

Place ice cubes in shaker
Add lime juice, grenadine and Cuban rum
Shake well and strain
Pour into cocktail glass
Garnish with lemon and cherry on stick

Very similar to Daiquiri but gets its name from RON BACARDI – *the spirit used.*

*C*UBA LIBRE

RATIOS	**INGREDIENTS**
1½	1½ × 25ml rum (dark)
1	1 × 25ml lemon juice
10	250ml Coca-Cola
	1 lemon slice, 4 ice cubes, 2 straws

PREPARATION

Place ice cubes in highball glass
Add rum, Coca-Cola and lemon juice
Stir
Add lemon slice
Serve with straws

Popularised during Prohibition by Americans who could afford to hop over from Florida to Havana.

*D*AIQUIRI

RATIOS	**INGREDIENTS**
1	1 × 50ml rum (white)
	4 dashes gomme (sugar syrup)
1	juice of 2 limes
	crushed ice
	1 cocktail cherry, 1 lime slice, 1 cocktail stick

PREPARATION

Fill shaker ¾ full with crushed ice

Add rum, sugar syrup and lime juice

Shake well

Strain into Martini glass

Garnish with cherry on stick and lime

Named after the Daiquiri Nickel Mine, Cuba where it was invented for American engineers during a shortage of imported liquor.

*P*INACOLADA

RATIOS	INGREDIENTS
1	1 × 25ml rum
2	1 × 50ml coconut cream
4	11.3cl ounces pineapple juice
	10 ice cubes, 1 cocktail stick
	1 pineapple chunk
	slither of fresh coconut

PREPARATION

Place ice in shaker
Add rum, coconut cream and pineapple juice
Shake well and strain
Serve in chilled highball glass
Garnish with coconut and pineapple on stick

*P*LANTER'S PUNCH

RATIOS	INGREDIENTS
1	1 × 25ml rum
3	60ml orange juice
3	60ml pineapple juice
	2 barspoons grenadine, 10 ice cubes
	1 cocktail stick, 1 orange slice
	1 pineapple chunk

PREPARATION

Place ice in shaker

Add rum and orange juice, pineapple juice and grenadine

Shake well and strain

Serve in chilled highball glass

Garnish with orange slice and pineapple chunk on stick

*R*UM COLLINS

RATIOS	INGREDIENTS
3	1½ × 25ml rum (white)
3	1½ × 25ml lemon juice
2	1 × 25ml gomme (sugar syrup)
	1 lemon slice
	1 cocktail cherry, 1 cocktail stick, 4–5 ice cubes
	2 straws, soda

PREPARATION

Place ice cubes in shaker
Add lemon juice, sugar syrup and rum
Shake well. Do not strain
Pour into chilled Collins glass
Top up with soda and stir
Garnish with lemon slice and cocktail cherry on stick
Serve with straws

ZOMBIE VOODOO

RATIOS	INGREDIENTS
2	1 × 25ml rum (golden)
2	1 × 25ml rum (white)
1	½ × 25ml rum (dark)
2	1 × 25ml lime juice
2	1 × 25ml orange juice
	3 drops Angostura bitters
1	½ × 25ml gomme (sugar syrup)
	1 egg white, ice cubes, 1 pineapple chunk
	2 straws, 1 orange slice, 1 lemon slice
	1 cocktail cherry and stick, 1 sprig of mint

PREPARATION

Fill shaker ½ full with ice cubes

Add rums, juices, sugar syrup, egg white and Angostura bitters

Shake well. Do not strain. Pour into Collins glass

Garnish with fruit slices, pineapple, cherry and mint

*B*LACK RUSSIAN

RATIOS
2
1

INGREDIENTS
1 × 25ml vodka
½ × 25ml Kahlúa
ice cubes

PREPARATION
Place ice cubes into lowball glass
Add ingredients
Stir well

*B*LOODY MARY

RATIOS	**INGREDIENTS**
1	1 × 50ml vodka
2	11.3cl tomato juice
	2 dashes Worcestershire sauce, 1 dash Tabasco sauce
	2 dashes Angostura bitters, juice of ½ lemon
	pinch of salt and pepper, celery stick, lemon slice
	1 straw, 5 ice cubes

PREPARATION

Place ice cubes in shaker
Add vodka, tomato juice, Worcester sauce, lemon juice,
Tabasco sauce, Angostura Bitters, salt and pepper
Shake well and strain. Serve into a highball glass
Garnish with celery, lemon slice over rim of glass and straw

❖❖

*Invented by Fernard Petiot working in Harry's New York Bar, Paris in
1920s and named after Mary Pickford, actress of the Thirties.*

*C*AVENDISH

RATIOS
1
2½

INGREDIENTS
2 × 25ml vodka
120ml champagne
2 dashes Angostura bitters
1 lemon slice
crushed ice

PREPARATION
Fill a highball glass with crushed ice
Add Angostura bitters and vodka
Top up with champagne
Garnish with lemon slice
Serve immediately

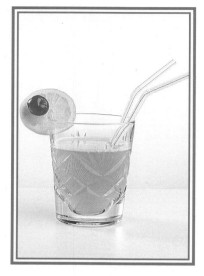

$\mathscr{F}$ORESTER

RATIOS	INGREDIENTS
3	1½ × 25ml vodka
1	½ × 25ml sweet vermouth
1	½ × 25ml dry vermouth
	½ teaspoon grenadine
1	juice of ½ grapefruit
	4 ice cubes, 1 lemon slice, 1 cocktail cherry
	1 cocktail stick, straws

PREPARATION

Place ice cubes in shaker

Add grapefruit juice, grenadine, vodka and sweet and dry vermouths

Shake well and strain

Pour into chilled old fashioned glass

Garnish with lemon and cherry on stick

Serve with straws

*H*ARVEY WALLBANGER

RATIOS	**INGREDIENTS**
2	1 × 25ml vodka
1	½ × 25ml Galliano
20	250ml orange juice
	5 ice cubes (shaker), 2 ice cubes (glass)
	1 orange slice
	straw and stirrer

PREPARATION

Place ice cubes in shaker
Add vodka and orange juice
Shake well and strain into highball glass
Add 2 ice cubes. Float Galliano on top
Garnish with slice of orange, straw and stirrer

*I*NSPIRATION

RATIOS	INGREDIENTS
4	2 × 25ml vodka
1	½ × 25ml Benedictine
1	½ × 25ml dry vermouth
	1 lemon slice
	1 cocktail cherry, 5 ice cubes

PREPARATION

Place ice cubes in bar glass
Add Benedictine, dry vermouth and vodka
Stir well and strain
Pour into chilled Paris goblet or champagne saucer
Garnish with lemon slice and cherry on stick

$\mathcal{M}$OSCOW MULE

RATIOS	INGREDIENTS
3	1½ × 25ml vodka
20	250ml ginger beer
1	½ × 25ml lemon juice
	5–6 ice cubes, 1 lemon slice, 1 cucumber slice

PREPARATION

Place ice cubes in shaker
Add vodka and lemon juice. Shake well and strain
Pour into chilled highball glass
Add slices of lemon and cucumber
Top up with ginger beer. Stir and serve

Named after Smirnoff's factory in Moscow and produced in Los Angeles in 1947 by John Martin. Served in a special copper mug as a gimmick.

*S*CREWDRIVER

RATIOS | **INGREDIENTS**
1 | 1 × 50ml vodka
2 | 11.3cl orange juice
| crushed ice, 1 orange slice
| 1 cocktail cherry

PREPARATION

Fill shaker ¼ full with crushed ice
Add vodka and orange juice
Shake well
Strain into old fashioned glass
Garnish with orange slice and cherry on stick

Another gimmick drink produced by John Martin using vodka; it soon became a craze which has survived.

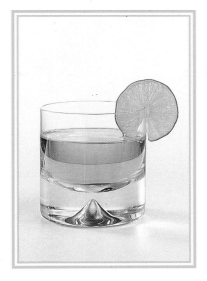

*B*ENEDICT

RATIOS	INGREDIENTS
3	1½ × 25ml whisky
1	½ × 25ml Benedictine
4	50ml ginger ale
	lime slice
	2 ice cubes

PREPARATION

Place ice cubes in bar glass
Add whisky and Benedictine and stir well
Pour all into old fashioned glass
Top up with ginger ale
Garnish with lime slice

*B*RAINSTORM

RATIOS	INGREDIENTS
1	1 × 25ml whisky
1	1 × 25ml dry vermouth
1	1 × 25ml Benedictine
	1 orange slice
	2 tablespoons crushed ice

PREPARATION

Place crushed ice in bar glass
Add whisky, dry vermouth and Benedictine
Stir well and strain
Pour into chilled tulip glass
Garnish with orange slice

ℰDINBURGH

RATIOS	**INGREDIENTS**
6	1½ × 25ml whisky
1	¼ × 25ml apricot brandy
1	¼ × 25ml crème de menthe
2	½ × 25ml dry vermouth
	2 dashes Angostura bitters
	5 ice cubes
	mint

PREPARATION

Place 4 ice cubes in bar glass
Shake in Angostura bitters
Add whisky, apricot brandy, crème de menthe, and dry
vermouth
Stir very well. Strain into lowball glass
Garnish with mint and ice cube

*G*ALLIANO SOUR

RATIOS	**INGREDIENTS**
2	1 × 25ml whisky
2	1 × 25ml Galliano
2	1 × 25ml orange juice
1	½ × 25ml lemon juice
	5–6 ice cubes
	1 orange wheel

PREPARATION

Place ice cubes in shaker
Add whisky, Galliano, lemon and orange juice
Shake well and strain
Pour into frosted sour glass (frost with sugar)
Garnish with orange wheel

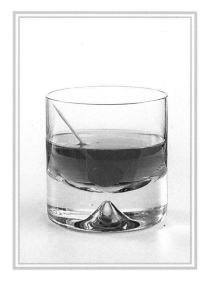

*M*ANHATTAN

RATIOS	INGREDIENTS
3	1½ × 25ml whisky
1	½ × 25ml sweet vermouth
	5 ice cubes, 1 cocktail cherry, 1 cocktail stick

PREPARATION
Place ice cubes in bar glass
Add sweet vermouth and whisky
Stir well and strain. Pour into chilled lowball glass or old–
fashioned glass
Add cocktail cherry on stick

*Originally invented in Maryland using sugar syrup instead of vermouth
to revive a duellist in 1846, New York. In the 1890s sweet vermouth
replaced the sugar syrup and the drink was named after the locality.*

*O*LD FASHIONED

INGREDIENTS
1 × 25ml rye whisky
2 drops Angostura bitters
1 × sugar cube
2 × ice cubes
1 × slice of orange

PREPARATION
Place sugar cube into lowball glass
Add Angostura bitters to sugar
Crush sugar cube
Add ice cubes, then orange slice and whisky
Stir

*R*OB ROY

RATIOS	**INGREDIENTS**
3	1½ × 25ml whisky
1	½ × 25ml sweet vermouth
	1 cocktail cherry
	1 cocktail stick
	7 ice cubes

PREPARATION

Place ice cubes in bar glass
Add whisky and sweet vermouth
Stir well and strain
Serve in chilled Martini glass
Garnish with cocktail cherry on stick

*S*COTCH MIST

INGREDIENTS
2 × 25ml whisky
1 sprig of mint
crushed ice
2 short straws

PREPARATION
Fill old fashioned glass ¾ full with crushed ice
Place mint leaves on ice
Pour on whisky and stir
Serve with 2 short straws

*W*HISKY SOUR

RATIOS	**INGREDIENTS**
4	1 × 50ml whisky
4	1 × 50ml lemon juice
1	6 dashes gomme (sugar syrup)
	crushed ice, 1 orange slice
	1 cocktail cherry
	1 cocktail stick

PREPARATION

Fill shaker ¾ full with crushed ice
Add whisky, lemon juice and sugar syrup
Shake well and strain
Serve in sour glass
Garnish with orange slice and cocktail cherry on stick

AMERICAN GLORY

RATIOS	INGREDIENTS
5	120ml champagne
1	juice of ½ orange
1	25ml soda
	1 orange slice, 2 ice cubes

PREPARATION

Place ice cubes in highball glass
Add orange juice and champagne
Top with soda
Garnish with orange slice

*B*LACK VELVET

RATIOS   **INGREDIENTS**
1   ½ glass champagne
1   ½ glass Guinness (stout)

PREPARATION
Fill a Paris goblet or Irish coffee glass with equal quantities of
stout and champagne
Should be drunk as soon as possible

BUCKS FIZZ

RATIOS	**INGREDIENTS**
2	⅔ glass sparkling wine
1	⅓ glass orange juice
	1 orange slice
	1 cocktail cherry
	1 cocktail stick

PREPARATION
Place orange juice in chilled champagne saucer
Top up with chilled sparkling wine
Garnish with orange slice and cherry on stick
Serve immediately

*The Englishman's version of Champagne à l'Orange as served by
Bucks Club in London.*

*C*HAMPAGNE COCKTAIL

INGREDIENTS
120ml champagne
1 teaspoon brandy, 1 sugar cube
2 dashes Angostura bitters, 1 orange slice
1 cocktail cherry, 1 cocktail stick

PREPARATION
Place sugar cube into champagne saucer
Splash Angostura bitters onto cube
Add champagne
Float brandy on top
Garnish with orange slice and cherry on stick

K'IR ROYALE

INGREDIENTS
Chilled sparkling wine
2 dashes crème de cassis

PREPARATION
Place crème de cassis in well chilled champagne saucer
Top up with chilled sparkling wine

*Canon Kir, when Parish Priest at Nolay, decided to add crème de cassis
to white Burgundy. Today champagne, sparkling wine or sparkling
white Burgundy is used.*

*S*ANGRIA

RATIOS	INGREDIENTS
5	125ml red table wine
1	1 × 25ml brandy
2	1 × 50ml orange juice
4	11.3cl lemonade
	cut oranges, cut lemon
	3 ice cubes (glass), ice for bar glass

PREPARATION

Place ice cubes and cut fruit in highball glass
Place ice cubes in bar glass and add wine
Add orange juice and brandy
Add lemonade and stir to blend
Strain into chilled glass

Traditional Spanish drink.

$\mathcal{A}$MERICANO

RATIOS	**INGREDIENTS**
1	1 × 25ml Campari
2	1 × 50ml sweet vermouth
	soda, 1 orange slice or lemon twist
	6 ice cubes

PREPARATION

Place ice cubes in bar glass
Add Campari and vermouth
Stir well
Strain into old fashioned glass
Top with soda and stir
Garnish with orange slice or lemon twist

Name derived from American style Americano.

*A*PPLEKNOCKER

RATIOS	INGREDIENTS
2	2 × 25ml Galliano
1	1 × 25ml lemon juice
10	250ml apple juice
	1 lemon slice, 1 apple slice
	5 ice cubes (for shaker)
	2 ice cubes (for glass)

PREPARATION

Place ice cubes in shaker
Add Galliano and lemon juice
Shake well and strain into highball glass
Add ice cubes
Top up with apple juice
Garnish with lemon juice and apple slices

*E*GG NOGG

RATIOS	INGREDIENTS
	1 whole egg
1	1 × 50ml sherry (or any desired spirit)
	½ teaspoon powdered sugar
2½	125ml milk
	strawberry
	nutmeg

PREPARATION

Into shaker place egg, powdered sugar, sherry and milk
Shake well
Strain into highball glass
Garnish with strawberry
Grate a little nutmeg on top

*F*ERNET BRANCA

RATIOS	**INGREDIENTS**
1	1 × 25ml Fernet Branca
	1 dash Pernod
3	60ml iced water
	2 cherries, 3 ice cubes

PREPARATION
Place ice cubes in old fashioned glass
Pour on Fernet Branca, Pernod and iced water
Garnish with cherries
Drink in one go!

Ideal for hangover — medicinal flavour and aroma.

*M*ARGARITA

RATIOS	INGREDIENTS
2	1 × 25ml Tequila
1	½ × 25ml Cointreau
1	½ × 25ml fresh lime juice
	ice cubes, lemon juice, salt

PREPARATION
Dip the glass rim in lemon juice and redip in salt
½ fill shaker with ice cubes
Add all ingredients. Shake well
Strain into ready prepared cocktail glass

Invented by a Mexican bartender in Virginia City, USA. Named after his girlfriend, who was accidentally shot in a street shooting and died in his arms.

*P*IMMS No 1

RATIOS	**INGREDIENTS**
1	1 × 50ml Pimms
4	180ml lemonade
	4 ice cubes
	Fruit: 1 orange slice, 1 lemon slice, 1 cucumber slice, cucumber peel, 1 apple slice, 1 strawberry, bee-borage, 1 sprig mint, 2 straws

PREPARATION

Place Pimms in highball glass or Pimms glass
Add ice cubes and fruit. Top up with lemonade
Garnish with fruit, mint and bee-borage. Serve with straws

❧❧❧

The recipe for the world's first Gin Sling was invented by James Pimms of Pimms' Oyster Bar, near the City of London. The world famous Pimms No 1 cup is based on fine gin and other secret ingredients.

*T*EQUILA SUNRISE

RATIOS	INGREDIENTS
1	1 × 25ml Tequila
3	3 × 25ml orange juice
	2 barspoons grenadine, 10 ice cubes
	1 orange slice, 1 cocktail cherry, 1 cocktail stick

PREPARATION

Place ice cubes in shaker. Add Tequila and orange juice
Shake well. Strain mixture into chilled Martini or highball glass
Slowly pour in grenadine
Allow to settle. Garnish with orange and cherry on stick
Just before serving stir once.

Name taken from early Spanish settlement in Mexico where a distillery to make spirit from a national brew was established. Sunrise is the visual effect of the drink.

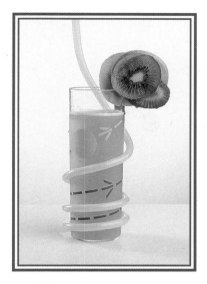

*F*RUIT CUP

RATIOS	**INGREDIENTS**
1	2 × 50ml orange juice
1	2 × 50ml grapefruit juice
1	2 × 50ml pineapple juice
1	2 × 50ml apple juice
	1 slice of apple, 1 slice of lemon
	1 slice of orange, 1 kiwi fruit
	1 strawberry, straws

PREPARATION

Fill shaker ¾ full with ice cubes
Add all fruit juice. Shake well
Pour into highball glass
Decorate with apple, lemon and orange slices and strawberry
Serve with straws

*L*ASSI

INGREDIENTS
125ml plain yoghurt
1 tablespoon double cream
2 tablespoon castor sugar
1 teaspoon rose water
ice cubes

PREPARATION
Fill shaker ½ full of ice cubes
Add all ingredients
Shake well
Pour into chilled Martini glass

*P*ARSON'S SPECIAL

INGREDIENTS
11.3cl orange juice
1 egg yolk
2 teaspoon grenadine
soda water, ice cubes
1 slice kiwi fruit, 1 strawberry

PREPARATION
Fill shaker ¾ full with ice cubes
Add all ingredients
Shake well
Strain into lowball glass
Top up with soda water
Stir and garnish with kiwi fruit and strawberry

PRAIRIE OYSTER

INGREDIENTS
1 egg yolk, 1 dash Cayenne pepper
1 teaspoon Worcestershire sauce
1 teaspoon tomato ketchup
2 dashes vinegar

PREPARATION
Place all ingredients in Paris goblet and stir
To be drunk in one gulp!

A drink given to a sick invalid who requested oysters but was given egg yolks instead. He recovered!

*P*USSY FOOT

RATIOS	**INGREDIENTS**
2	1 × 50ml orange juice
2	1 × 50ml lemon juice
2	1 × 50ml lime juice
1	1 × 25ml grenadine
	1 egg yolk, crushed ice
	soda, 1 strawberry, 2 straws

PREPARATION

Fill shaker ¾ full with crushed ice
Add fruit juices, grenadine and egg yolk
Shake well and strain
Pour into highball glass. Top up with soda
Garnish with strawberry and straws

*R*AISIN & GINGER PUNCH

RATIOS	INGREDIENTS
4	11.3cl apple juice
4	11.3cl ginger ale
1	1 × 25ml lemon juice
	1 teaspoon clear honey
	1 teaspoon raisins, 2 lemon zest spirals
	sprigs of mint, lemon slices, crushed ice, 2 straws

PREPARATION

Fill shaker ¼ full with crushed ice

Add lemon juice and zest, honey, raisins and apple juice

Shake well. Pour ice and mixture into Collins glass

Add ginger ale. Stir well

Garnish with lemon slices, mint and straws

*S*T CLEMENT'S

RATIOS
1 × bottle
1 × bottle

INGREDIENTS
11.3cl orange juice
11.3cl bitter lemon
crushed ice, 1 lemon slice
1 orange slice, straw

PREPARATION
Fill shaker ¼ full crushed ice
Add orange juice
Shake well
Pour ice and orange juice into Collins glass
Add bitter lemon and stir
Decorate with lemon and orange slice
Serve with straw

*S*HIRLEY TEMPLE

RATIOS
1 × bottle

INGREDIENTS
11.3cl ginger ale
1 teaspoon grenadine
cocktail cherries
8 ice cubes
straws

PREPARATION
Place ice cubes into highball glass
Add ginger ale
Add grenadine
Stir slightly
Garnish with cherries and straws

𝒯EA PUNCH

RATIOS	INGREDIENTS
3	75ml cold tea
4	11.3cl orange juice
1	1 × 25ml lemon juice
2	1 × 50ml raspberry juice
2	1 × 50ml pineapple juice
	soda water, ice cubes
	1 orange slice, 1 lemon slice

PREPARATION

Fill shaker ½ full ice cubes
Add tea and fruit juices
Shake well. Place in highball glass
Top up with soda water
Garnish with fruit slices

*Y*ELLOW DWARF

RATIOS	**INGREDIENTS**
	1 egg yolk
1	1 × 50ml cream
1	1 × 50ml orgeat syrup
	maraschino cherry
	ice cubes
	soda

PREPARATION

Fill shaker ½ full with ice cubes
Add egg yolk, cream and orgeat syrup
Shake well
Strain into cocktail glass
Top up with soda
Garnish with cherry

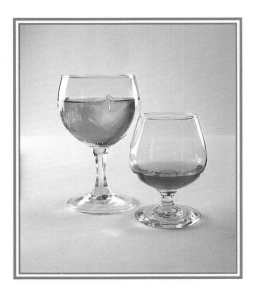

BAR DRINKS

Contents

Preparation of bar for service

Stock

- Check and stock up wines, spirits, vermouths, liqueurs, mineral waters, fruit juices and cordials
- Store stock at the correct temperatures ready for service

Glassware

- Steam clean sufficient quantity of all glassware and have ready to hand (see page 146 for illustrations)

Equipment

- Ensure all equipment is clean
- Keep bar top tidy and uncluttered, as it will be on view to customers
- Prepare:
  > Ice buckets, wine baskets, sideplates and doyleys, salvers, ice tongs, fruit tongs and measures
  > Liqueur trolley if applicable
  > Water jugs with ice

Miscellaneous

- Prepare all garnishes
- Ensure ancillary items are readily available:
  > salvas, straws, matches, cocktail sticks, ice cubes, crushed ice, corkscrew, clean napkins, cut fruit, cocktail cherries, sugar, cruet set and Worcestershire sauce, tabasco sauce, Angostura bitters

Drinks list

- Check for cleanliness, up to date and correct information
- Place promotional material in prominent positions

During service

- At the start of service, wash your hands
- Ensure perfect personal presentation and hygiene
- All drinks issued require written documentation
- No written check – No drinks
- Prepare:
  customers's orders in strict rotation
  drinks on bar top in full view of customers
  as per photograph, with due regard to hygiene
- Always:
  use the correct measure and fill the measure to the top
  hold glasses by the stem
  use tongs for ice and fruit slices and garnishes
  pour drinks so the customer can see the label
- Place all drinks on a clean salver with a serviette for service at table or reception area
- Always provide clean glass for a repeat drink order (except repeat bottled wine served at table)
- Tidy up as you work

After service

- Always leave the bar as you would wish to find it
- Clean and tidy bar
- Wash and stack glasses
- Empty rubbish bin
- Book out stock sold
- Replenish stock used
- Ensure the security of the bar at all times

Aperitifs

Aperitifs are alcoholic drinks offered before a meal to 'whet' or sharpen the appetite. Aperitif covers a number of drinks used as appetisers, and most contain aromatic herbs to stimulate the palate. These drinks can be spirit-based such as Campari, or wine-based such as Vermouths. Vermouth is wine flavoured with herbs and other substances. Flavourings commonly used are orange and lemonpeels, quinine, cloves, coriander, liquorice and other roots and flowers. The flower 'wormwood' gives its name to Vermouth through its German name *wermut*.

Spirit-based Aperitifs or 'Bitters' are spirits flavoured with roots, barks and herbs and can be served as a drink e.g. Campari, or used to flavour drinks, e.g. Angostura.

As well as Vermouths, Bitters, Fortified wines (such as Sherries, Madeira) and Pernod are categorised as aperitifs.

Spirits

Spirits are drinks of high alcoholic strength made by distillation. Spirits can be made from any fermentable base, such as fruit juice, sugar solution, grain, vegetables. They can be served on their own or with a mixer for a long drink.

Liqueurs

Liqueurs or Digestif aid digestion and are offered at the end of a meal. Liqueurs consist of a spirit, flavoured with fruits, herbs, roots, flowers, beans or kernels, and sweetened with sugar, syrup, honey and sometimes colourings. Some liqueurs originated from secret recipes and were produced by the monks at Benedictine, Chartreuse for medicinal purposes. Other liqueurs are fruit based like Cherry Brandy. All liqueurs are strong alcoholic drinks.

Liqueurs can be displayed and served from a liqueur trolley within a restaurant, ensuring the labels of the liqueurs face the customer. They can be served frappe for flavour enhancement and to dilute the drink.

Beer / cider / perry

Beer

Beers are fermented drinks made from malted barley. There are 3 basic types of beer:

- Ales:
  > Pale
  > Dark
  > Strong
- Stouts:
  > Sweet
  > Bitter
- Lager

Beer can be draught, bottled or canned. There are also low alcohol and non-alcoholic beers available.

Cider

Cider is an alcoholic drink produced from the fermentation of apple juice. It is available draught, bottled or canned. The alcoholic strength varies, and it can be sweet or dry, sparkling, carbonated, or still.

Perry

Perry is an alcoholic drink produced from the fermentation of pear juice. Perry can be dry or sweet and sparkling.

Wine

Wine is the alcoholic beverage obtained from the juice of freshly gathered grapes, the fermentation of which is carried out in the district of origin according to local habit and tradition.

Wine may be classified:

- by colour: Red, Rosé, White
- by taste: sweet, medium, dry
- by strength: table, fortified
- by style: still, sparkling
- by age: vintage, non-vintage

Wine should be served at the correct temperature:
red wines should be served room temperature
rose wines and white wines served cool
sparkling wines and sweet white served chilled

Wine sold by the glass must be measured 125ml, whereas wine sold by the bottle for service at the table requires:

- Adjustment of glasses if applicable
- Presentation of bottle
- Removal of cork
- Taster to host
- Serve all guests first
- Serve host last
- Top-up wine glasses as required

Minerals

Juices

Fresh fruit juice requires a fruit press or juice squeezer to extract the juice efficiently. Fruit juice can be bottled, canned or cartons and in all cases requires shaking before opening. Tomato juice cocktail is ready bottled, mixed with Worcestershire sauce.

Cordials/syrups

Cordials can be diluted to produce a long drink or used in mixed drinks.

Squashes

Squashes are diluted with iced water or soda water to provide a long cool drink.

Aerated waters

Aerated waters or artificial mineral waters are flavoured water which is carbonated to produce an effervescent drink. They are usually clear except for Bitter Lemon. Aerated waters can be served on their own or used as a 'mixer' with other drinks.

Natural mineral waters

Natural mineral water obtained naturally from the ground and bottled at source can be still or sparkling. They are often drunk for health and medicinal purposes. No ice (tap water) should be served in natural mineral waters but the taste benefits from chilling.

Speciality coffee

Speciality coffees can be produced using any spirit or liqueur selected by the customer. The following are a list of the more popular speciality coffees:

Cafe Royale:	Cognac
Cafe Parisienne:	Brandy
Cafe Calypso:	Tia Maria
Cafe Caribbean:	Rum
Cafe Monks:	Benedictine
Cafe Prince Charles:	Drambuie
Cafe Gaelic:	Scotch Whisky
Cafe Irish:	Irish Whiskey
Cafe Witches:	Strega

A 'Floater' coffee can be served as for Speciality coffee with the omission of the liqueur or spirit.

∅UBONNET

Glass: 6⅔ Paris Goblet
Measure: 50ml
Garnish: Ice, lemon slice

NOTES

Can be served with lemonade or soda as requested.
Available Dubonnet Rouge or Blond (sweet red or white wine with a hint of quinine).

*C*AMPARI

Glass: 6⅔ Paris Goblet
Measure: 25ml
Garnish: Ice, orange slice

NOTES

Can be served with soda water or orange juice as requested,
using a 10oz Slim Jim glass.

Campari is an Italian spirit-based aperitif with a hint of orange
zest and quinine.

*P*ERNOD

Glass: 6⅔ Paris Goblet
Measure: 25ml
Garnish: Iced water

NOTES
A clear bright yellow drink which turns 'milky' on the addition of water.
Classified as a 'Pastis' which is a generic name for Anis or liquorice flavoured spirits.

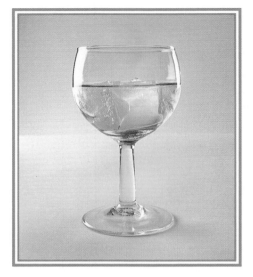

⏁HITE PORT

Glass: 6⅔ Paris Goblet
Measure: 50ml
Garnish: Ice cubes

NOTES
Serve white port as above when requested as an aperitif.
White port can be served in a port glass without ice if
accompanying food.

FORTIFIED WINES

$\mathscr{M}$ADEIRA

Glass: Copita
Measure: 50ml

NOTES
There are 4 main types of Madeira: Sercial (Dry), Verdelho
(Medium), Bual (rich, sweet), Malmsey (very sweet).
The Madeira wines are named after the grapes used.

ℐHERRY

Glass: Copita
Measure: 50ml

NOTES

Serve Dry sherry chilled; Medium and Sweet sherry at room temperature.

Sherry is produced in Spain, and only Spanish sherry can be sold as 'Sherry'.

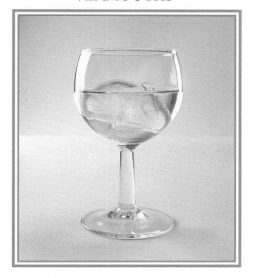

*I*TALIAN BIANCO

Glass: 6⅔ Paris Goblet
Measure: 50ml
Garnish: Ice, slice lemon

$\mathcal{I}$TALIAN ROSSO

Glass: 6⅔ Paris Goblet
Measure: 50ml
Garnish: Cherry on stick

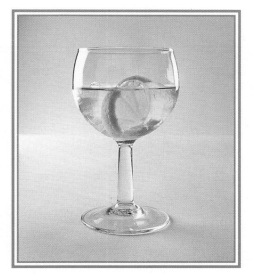

𝒩OILLY PRAT

Glass: 6⅔ Paris Goblet
Measure: 50ml
Garnish: Ice, slice lemon

JUICES

𝒻RUIT JUICE

Glass: Club Goblet
Measure: by glass
Garnish: slice of appropriate fruit

NOTES
Fruit juice should be well chilled and shaken well before
opening bottles, cans or cartons.

ℱRESH FRUIT JUICE

Glass: Club Goblet presented on a sideplate and doyley, with teaspoon
Measure: by glass
Garnish: Castor sugar offered in a coupe

NOTES
Fruit used for freshly squeezed fruit juice should be of the finest quality.

*T*OMATO JUICE

Glass: Club Goblet presented on a sideplate and doyley, with teaspoon
Measure: by glass
Garnish: Worcestershire Sauce, cruet set on sideplate and doyley

SQUASHES AND CORDIALS

*O*RANGE

Glass: 12oz Worthington
Measure: 2 × 50ml
Garnish: Ice, orange slices, straws

NOTES
Top up with iced water or soda water.

*L*IME

Glass: 12oz Worthington
Measure: 2 × 50ml
Garnish: Ice, lime slices, straws

NOTES
Top up with iced water or soda water.

AERATED WATERS

_T_ONIC WATER

Glass: 6⅔ Paris Goblet
Measure: by glass
Garnish: Ice, lemon slice

NOTES
Serve chilled.
Tonic Water is flavoured with quinine and can be served to
accompany spirits, e.g. Gin and Tonic.
Slimline Tonic served as above.

*B*ITTER LEMON

Glass: 6⅔ Paris Goblet
Measure: by glass
Garnish: Ice, lemon slice

NOTES
Serve chilled.
Can be served as a mixer to accompany spirits e.g. Gin and
Bitter Lemon.

ⅅRY GINGER

Glass: 6⅔ Paris Goblet
Measure: by glass

NOTES
Serve chilled.
Can be served as a mixer to accompany spirits e.g. Brandy and
Ginger.

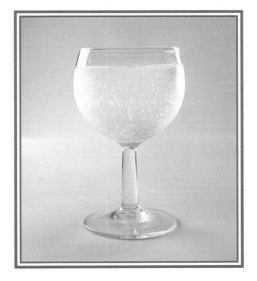

✐ODA WATER

Glass: 6⅔ Paris Goblet
Measure: by glass

NOTES
Serve well chilled.
Can be served as a mixer e.g. Whisky and Soda.

ℒEMONADE

Glass: 10oz Slim Jim
Measure: by glass
Garnish: Ice, lemon slice

NOTES
Serve well chilled. Can be used as a mixer with spirits, juices or squashes.

𝒞OLA

Glass: 10oz Slim Jim
Measure: by glass
Garnish: ice, lemon slice

NOTES
Serve well chilled. Can be used as a mixer for spirits e.g. Bacardi and Coke.
Diet Cokes served as above.

NATURAL MINERAL WATERS

✐ERRIER

Glass: 8oz Slim Jim
Measure: by glass
Garnish: slice lemon

NOTES

Serve well chilled, with no ice. If served at the table the bottle should be opened in front of the guest and served into a Paris Goblet at the table.

✍ALVERN

Glass: 8oz Slim Jim
Measure: by glass

NOTES

Serve well chilled with no ice.
If served at the table the bottle should be opened at the table and served into Paris Goblets at the table.

𝒢UINNESS

Glass: 12oz Worthington
Measure: by glass

NOTES

Serve chilled. To serve start by pouring the Guinness down the side of the glass and straighten glass to give a 'head'.

ℒIGHT ALE

Glass: 12oz Worthington
Measure: by glass

NOTES
Serve chilled.
To serve start by pouring the Light Ale down the side of the
glass and straighten glass to give a 'head'.
Low alcohol beers are served in the same manner.

ℒAGER

Glass: Pilsner
Measure: by glass

NOTES

Serve chilled.

To serve start by pouring the Lager down the side of the glass and straighten glass to give a 'head'.

For Lager and Lime add 25ml Lime to the glass before adding the Lager.

CIDER

Glass: 12oz Worthington
Measure: by glass

NOTES
Serve chilled.

𝓑EER DRAUGHT

Glass: ½ or 1 pint Beer Mug
Measure: by glass

NOTES
Serve chilled. The 'head' does not count as part of the ½ pint or 1 pint Beer.

𝒮HANDY

Glass: 12oz Worthington
Measure: by glass

NOTES
Prepared by half filling glass with Lemonade and topping up
with Bitter, Light Ale or Lager as ordered.

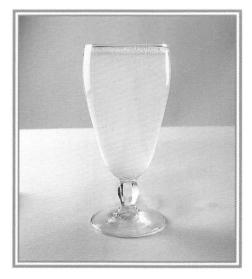

𝒢INGER BEER

Glass: 12oz Worthington
Measure: by glass

NOTES
Serve chilled. Ginger Beer could also be served in a 10oz Slim Jim.

*P*ERRY (BABYCHAM)

Glass: Champagne Saucer
Measure: by glass

NOTES
Serve chilled.

$\mathscr{A}$PPLE JUICE

Glass: 8oz Slim Jim
Measure: by glass
Garnish: apple slice (if available)

NOTES
Serve well chilled.

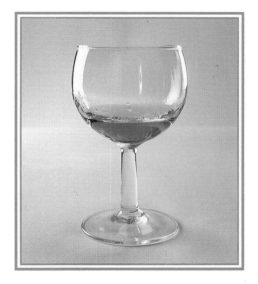

ЈOUTHERN COMFORT

Glass: 6⅔ Paris Goblet
Measure: 25ml

NOTES

Serve neat unless ice, soda water, iced water, or ginger ale requested (see page 128).

*Ƒ*COTCH WHISKY
*Ƒ*RISH WHISKEY

Glass: 6⅔ Paris Goblet
Measure: 25ml

NOTES

Serve neat unless ice, soda water, iced water, or ginger ale
requested (see page 127).
Bourbon Whisky is from America. Rye Whisky is made in
Canada and America.
Whisky Mac is Whisky served as above with the addition of
ginger wine.

*G*IN

Glass: 6⅔ Paris Goblet
Measure: 25ml
Garnish: Ice, lemon slice

NOTES

Often served with a mixer e.g. Gin and Tonic water, Gin and
Bitter Lemon as a long drink (use 10oz Slim Jim).

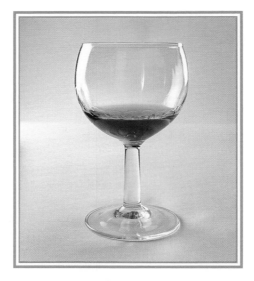

*R*UM

Glass: 6⅔ Paris Goblet
Measure: 25ml

NOTES

Can be served with a mixer e.g. Rum and Blackcurrant.

ℬACARDI

Glass: 6⅔ Paris Goblet/Slim Jim if long drink
Measure: 25ml

NOTES

Bacardi is usually served with an additional drink e.g. Bacardi
and Coke and as a long drink would be served in 10oz Slim Jim.

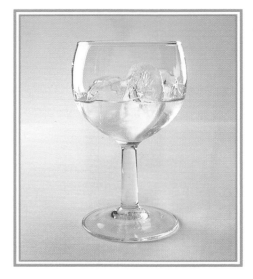

*V*ODKA

Glass: 6⅔ Paris Goblet
Measure: 25ml
Garnish: Ice, lemon slice

NOTES
Can be served with a mixer e.g. Vodka and Tonic.

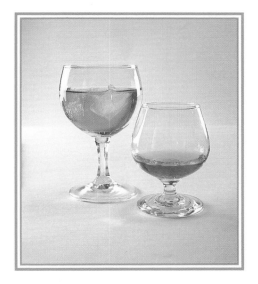

*B*RANDY

Glass: 6⅔ Paris Goblet
Measure: 25ml

NOTES

Served separately, or with a mixer as requested e.g. Brandy and
Ginger ale.

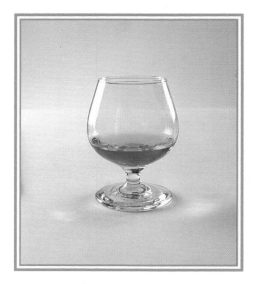

𝒞OGNAC

Glass: Brandy Balloon
Measure: 25ml

NOTES

A double Cognac would be served in a large Brandy Balloon to allow the Cognac to spread thinly in the glass, so the contents can be warmed by the customer cradling the glass in their hand.

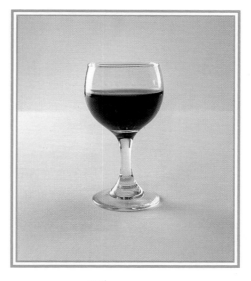

𝒫ORT

Glass: Port
Measure: 50ml

ᴀLL LIQUEURS

Glass: Liqueur
Measure: 25ml
Garnish: none except a coffee bean for Sambuca

*A*LL LIQUEURS FRAPPE

Glass: Copita
Measure: 25ml
Garnish: crushed ice, short straws

NOTES
Fill glass with crushed ice before adding the liqueur. Add shortened straws.

*A*LL SPECIALITY COFFEES

Glass: Paris Goblet
Measure: 25ml of chosen liqueur or spirit
Garnish: hot coffee and double cream; sideplate and doyley;
brown sugar.

PREPARATION

Warm glass
Add 1 teaspoon brown sugar and leave teaspoon in glass
Add hot black coffee
Stir until all sugar is dissolved
Add measure of liqueur or spirit of customer's choice
Pour double cream slowly over the back of teaspoon to float on
the coffee
Place glass onto sideplate and doyley

*C*HAMPAGNE OR SPARKLING WINE

Glass: Flute
Measure: by glass, by bottle

NOTES

Champagne or sparkling wine should be served well chilled.
For table service, present wine in icebucket on stand or on sideplate and doyley.
For service by the glass, pour slowly into flute glass and serve.
Reseal bottle with stopper.

MOSELLE AND ALSACE

Glass: green stemmed
Measure: by glass, by bottle

NOTES

Serve chilled. For table service, present wine in icebucket on stand or on sideplate and doyley.
Moselle and Alsace wines are bottled in green glass.

HOCK

Glass: brown stemmed
Measure: by glass, by bottle

NOTES

Serve chilled. For table service, present wine in icebucket on stand or on a sideplate and doyley.
Hock wine is bottled in brown glass.

*W*HITE WINE

Glass: white wine
Measure: by bottle

NOTES
Serve chilled. For table service, present wine in icebucket on stand or on sideplate and doyley. See page 95 for serving instructions.

*R*OSÉ WINE

Glass: Paris goblet
Measure: by bottle

NOTES
Serve chilled. For table service, present wine in icebucket on stand or on a sideplate and doyley. See page 95 for serving instructions.

*R*ED WINE

Glass: red wine
Measure: by bottle

NOTES
Serve at room temperature. For table service, present red wine in wine basket.

See page 95 for serving instructions.

*W*INE BY GLASS

Glass: lined wine glass
Measure: 125ml

NOTES

Serve white or rosé wine chilled.

Serve red wine at room temperature.

Wine ordered should be poured up to the line on the lined glasses.

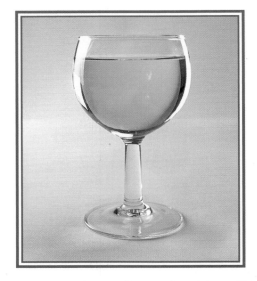

𝒟E-ALCOHOLISED WINE

Glass: Paris goblet
Measure: by glass, by bottle

NOTES

For table service, present wine in icebucket on stand or on sideplate and doyley.

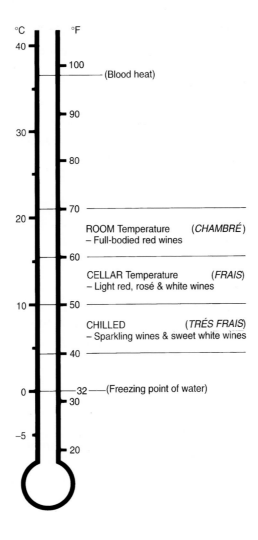

GLASSES

6⅔oz Paris Goblet

Water, spirits, Vermouths, aerated and mineral waters, aperitifs and speciality coffees

½ or pint Beer Mug

Draught beers

8oz Slim Jim

Aerated and mineral waters, apple juice

10oz Slim Jim

Carbonated drinks, spirits with mixers, Vermouth with mixer

$\mathscr{G}$LASSES

Tulip  Champagne, sparkling wine, cocktails

Club Goblet  Fruit juices

Copita  Sherry, Madeira, liqueur frappé

Saucer  Perry (Babycham)

$\mathcal{G}$LASSES

12oz Worthington

Beers, ciders, ginger beer, shandy, squashes and cordials

2oz Paris Goblet

Port or liqueur

Liqueur

Liqueurs

Brandy Balloon

After dinner brandy

Pilsner

Lager

GLASSES

Red Wine

Red wine by glass or bottle

Rosé Wine

Rosé wine by glass or bottle

White Wine

White wine sold by glass or bottle

Hock (brown stem)
Mosel (green stem)

German Hock
German Mosel